Contents

Contents

About the Authors

1

About the Authors

Dr John Mervyn-Smith
Co-Founder and Chief Psychologist of The GC Index

 John has over 30 years' experience of coaching senior leaders and their teams.

John's work in both clinical and occupational psychology underpins his understanding of the ways in which people make an impact at work. His extensive research in this field has led to the development of The GC Index®.

"Human beings have a fundamental drive to feel potent and to make a contribution to their world."

 www.linkedin.com/in/john-mervyn-smith-7337116

Nathan Ott
Co-Founder and Chief Polisher of The GC Index

Nathan has created a community that is committed to fostering the impact and contribution from everyone around the globe, whether they are a global Fortune CEO or a child in a developing country.

"Not everyone is a Game Changer, but everyone can make a game-changing impact."

www.linkedin.com/in/nathanott

Acknowledgements

2

Acknowledgements

**This book describes how The GC Index®
can be used to help people make an
impact.**

This work would not have been possible
without the advice and support of many
people. Foremost, we would like to thank
our immediate team for their support and
enthusiasm: Nicole Rogers, Operational
Polisher, Vicky Sleight, Chief Play Maker,
Andy Cracknell, Game Changer and Emma
Price, Game Changer/Polisher. We would
also like to thank our extended team
of proofreaders, Ana Ott, Hilary Mervyn-
Smith and Olivia Mervyn-Smith.

Thank you to our team of GCologists,
with a special thanks to all of those who
provide case studies. We would also
like to extend an enormous thank you
to Gaylin Jee, GCologist and Director of
33 Emeralds, who always finds time to
listen to our ideas and offer constructive
criticism, which has led to huge
improvements.

Those who contributed to this book
provided the perfect blend of knowledge
and skills that went into authoring,
designing and delivering the final version.

We would like to thank everyone who
has provided advice and offered views.
Whilst there are far too many people

involved to mention individually please know
we are hugely grateful for your support.

It's been fantastic to see so many people energised
by The GC Index® and wonderful to see the positive
impact it is having on both individuals' lives as well
as business and team performance.

Last, but by no means least a huge thank you to
Keshi Bouri, Creative Director at Keshi, who designed
the book and Emma Price, Director of Be Heard
Media. Emma has opened our eyes to explore new
ideas and challenged our thinking to improve the
quality and presentation.

Dr John Mervyn-Smith and Nathan Ott

11

Foreword

Foreword
by Adrian Furnham

 **All organisations seek out highly talented people who ensure the long-term success of the company. The question is how to define that relatively small group of identifiable people whose motivation and talent lead organisations to become and stay productive in a fast-changing world.**

These people are more than simply high flyers from the talent group. They are not just disruptive either. They seem to be different. They are called Game Changers. They don't play the game: they change it for everybody.

So how to spot a Game Changer? They seem to have lots of characteristics: creative and quirky; ambitious and a 'go-getter'; focused and also resilient; bright and they have vision.

A London based group led by Dr John Mervyn-Smith, an old friend and widely respected consultant, led this research. They found two factors or dimensions which characterised these people: Imagination and Obsession. What is interesting from a psychological perspective is that they don't often seem to "go together". From this insight we developed a test and a typology.

The team have come up with an unusual and unique tool, The GC Index®, which identifies preferences on these dimensions. People and organisations who have experienced it are seriously impressed. It is for many an "aha" experience which helps them understand themselves and others. It describes and explains the contributions of others at work and, which is the essence of this book, demonstrates how everyone can make a 'game-changing' impact.

Having helped us to recognise and understand Game Changers, The GC Index® has moved our thinking on by describing how innovation and transformational change is, in reality, not just a result of a few creative thinkers but the product of game-changing teams and cultures.

This book is a 'must read' for all those who are involved in the development of talent.

Adrian Furnham
Professor of Psychology

Introduction

Introduction

This book describes the ways in which everyone can make an impact as individuals, in a team and/or as part of an organisation. It offers a wealth of advice to Coaches and Managers, so that they can gain a deeper understanding of where they can support others in identifying how they can make an impact.

We pay particular attention to the role of a Coach in unleashing the impact an individual can make. You may be a Coach, currently being coached, or simply looking to maximise your own impact through the learnings you gain in this book. Whatever your reason for picking up this book, we guarantee you will have a better understanding of how you can maximise your own impact and the impact of others by the end of it.

Whether you are an Executive Coach, Sports Coach, or a Manager who seeks to get the best from others through coaching you have the opportunity to help and influence others. The coaching relationship is a privileged one: the Coach is in a position to bring their skills to bear to help someone change their lives and careers for the best. Necessarily, it is an intimate and intense relationship, often with much at stake.

The Coach owes it to their clients, and to themselves, to be the best that they can be. When they are, we are sure that all Coaches will attest to the fact that there is nothing more profoundly rewarding than helping someone, through insight and action, to feel more empowered and potent in their lives.

This book is an introduction to The GC Index® and, in particular, its value in a coaching context. For those of you accustomed to personality profiles and psychometrics of various sorts, The GC index® will feel familiar in the sense that it describes individual differences. However, rather than describing 'personality' it describes 'proclivities'; meaning The GC Index® describes individual differences when it comes to making an impact in a role, and as part of a team and organisation.

The philosophy underpinning The GC index® is a simple one, specifically that human beings strive to be potent in their world. You only need to watch the toddler learning to walk to see this, the determination to get up, again and again, after falling down. The drive for potency and, at times, mastery, is evident. Some might argue that this drive is a 'hard-wired' feature of our need as a species to survive, adapt and thrive.

What is clear is that people don't go to work to feel impotent. People thrive when they have a clarity of role and responsibility that allows them to make a valued contribution and impact. At the heart of effective performance at work is clarity of expectations and accurate feedback.

19

Consistent with this, The GC Index® looks at individual differences from the point of view of impact and contribution. It makes clear an individual's proclivity for making an impact in a way that 'plays to their strengths.'

The case studies, that make up the second half of this book, are presented by experienced Coaches. They demonstrate that when natural inclinations are recognised, harnessed and focused in the right way, people are at their most potent and valued at work. The GC Index® is a powerful tool that helps Coach and Coachee to do just that.

What we write about in this book can be applied when coaching anyone, regardless of level and industry. It is also relevant to individuals both inside and outside of work.

We hope you enjoy the read.

Dr John Mervyn-Smith and Nathan Ott

The Role of a Coach in the 21st Century

The Role of a Coach in the 21ˢᵗ Century

The role of a Coach, in the 21ˢᵗ Century, is to help organisations get the very best from their talent. A successful Coach will understand this context, they will understand the diverse nature of talent, how to understand, assess and develop it. They will be 'on top of' the latest thinking and practice in this regard.

Effective talent management in organisations includes an investment in succession planning, 'high potential' development, leadership development and talent development. Coaches can play a vital role in the success of these activities.

One approach to assessing talent!

Necessarily, there will be times when there is overlap across these activities: in sophisticated organisations, the talented individual who is seen as a potential CEO will form part of the succession plan and be groomed for future roles with the support of a variety of development initiatives.

Traditionally the approach has been one of defining what talent/leadership looks like, with development then being focused upon helping the individual to 'fit the mould', sculpting the 'perfect leader'. Over the last five decades a good deal of literature on the topic of leadership has reinforced this notion that there is a definitive and unitary view of leadership. We discuss this in more detail below.

The argument for doing this is an elegant one in some ways: 'Let's determine the characteristics of those individuals who have been successful within the organisation – those who have 'made it to the top' – and use that knowledge to create a leadership assessment framework against which we can assess our talent'.

However, there are a number of consequences of this approach.

Lack of diversity at senior levels within organisations

A one-dimensional view of leadership based upon those individuals who historically have been successful in an organisation has led to homogeneity at senior levels; reinforcing a notion of 'handsome is as handsome does'.

The phrase 'male, pale and stale' is often used to capture this picture of homogeneity. It is a vivid picture that suggests that such groups 'think as one' and 'act as one', that they lack diversity. Moreover, this 'people like us' approach will perpetuate and strengthen a set of norms that shape behaviours and organisational cultures for good.

The tendency of human beings to conform to what they see as accepted norms has been the focus of some fascinating and dramatic research and the pressure to conform in groups in particular, has also been the subject of a great deal of work, captured under the heading of 'Groupthink' (**1**).

A core theme in this work is the observation that individuals and groups, for a variety of reasons, seek to minimise difference and, with it, the potential for conflict. An absence of challenge and conflict serves to maintain the comfort of the status quo. Such conforming group cultures can be complacent and sterile; they stifle, consciously and unconsciously, the differences that can stimulate creative and transformational change.

Some organisations, such as Dyson, a British technology company, have taken a very different approach to the selection of their 'future leaders'. Their high potential talent is self-selected rather than a product of a 'top down' nominations approach which can reinforce homogeneity amongst senior leaders. Dyson's approach produced, as they had hoped, a diverse talent group, (as reflected in their aggregate profiles produced by The GC Index®), in terms of the group's individual and collective potential for impact and contribution to the business.

At first sight this approach may not seem that radical, but it is. Rather than the traditional approach to talent assessment and management: *This is what talents looks like, we will develop you to 'fit the mould,* the approach is one of: *Let's find out who our ambitious people are and develop their talents.*

> "Organisations continue to undervalue those talented individuals with no ambition to get to the top."

Neglected talent

Nurturing those individuals with the ambition for hierarchical success is an important part of talent management. However, there is a risk that organisations neglect those talented individuals with no ambition to get to the C-level. These individuals often don't get onto succession planning lists, they don't hit people's 'high potential' radar and they are not seen as leaders.

The result of this neglect has been illustrated by a review of data from The GC Index®. More specifically, our data, supported by interviews, shows that individuals with game-changing talent often struggle to settle in large corporations and leave to start their own businesses or join small ventures and start-ups. These individuals, by their very nature, resist the pressure to conform to what they see as the arbitrary rules and the bureaucracy that can stifle expression and, in turn the potential for creativity. When these 'different' individuals do survive and thrive in large corporations it is often because they have a boss who recognises their talent and gives them the support they need to express it.

Andrew Dyckhoff's case study, in the second half of this book, on page 85, brings to life the struggles that Game

Changers – those individuals who have original ideas and focus on turning them into reality – can have in organisations that don't fully appreciate their talents.

Encouragingly, successful organisations are increasingly aware that effective talent management also includes developing those talented individuals who have no ambition for hierarchical success, recognising that they can make a significant contribution to the success of an organisation.

Consider the story of BuroHappold, an international firm of engineering consultants. Their reputation, and success, has been built upon the creative, 'leading edge' quality of their work. Core to their success is a group of talented designers, many of whom have little interest in leading others or being future Partners in the firm. In this instance, the Global HR Director brought a clear, and practically useful distinction to the tasks of talent development, high potential development and succession planning. This enlightened HR leadership is not always so evident in corporate life.

Telefonica's Alpha project is another shining example of recognising and nurturing the diverse nature of talent critical to the success of the business. The aim of Alpha is to identify and bring to market creative, 'leading-edge' technologies and business models that have potential to change the world in different and significant ways.

Alpha brings creative minds together to develop teams to work on new innovations and leading-edge technology. To accelerate individual and collective impact, the team is working with The GC Index® language of game-changing impact into the entire talent lifecycle of 'Being an Alpha'. The GC Index® framework supports approaches to attracting talent, recruitment, development, performance management, team composition and community building.

Finally, Sammy Rashed's case study, on page 76, also shows how powerful the coaching relationship can be for people with Game Changer proclivities. It starts to demonstrate that in a climate where organisations are forced to change at an unprecedented rate the need to nurture this 'neglected talent' is critical. The GC Index® enables organisations to do just this with a language and framework for their people whereby 'Not everyone is a Game Changer but everyone can make a game-changing impact'.

Assumptions about talent and the role of the Coach

Coaches are often asked to work with people in ways that reflect assumptions about the nature of talent and talent development. Often this is of the form noted above: 'this is what talent looks like', can you help this individual to conform to this picture. The focus then,

Pic: Shutterstock

27

"Corporations tend to have development plans focusing on employees' areas of improvements"

is more upon 'fixing' weaknesses rather than building strengths.

So, for example, the request to coach a talented Finance Director to become 'more strategic' as she transitions into the CFO role, highlights some of the complex stakeholder dynamics that the effective Coach needs to manage at the outset of a coaching assignment.

Coaches can feel a pressure to collude with such a request. The effective Coach will be prepared to 'have the conversation', to challenge assumptions and expectations. They will explore the evidence for the apparent need for the CFO to be a strategic thinker – is this just a product of a fixed view of what C-level leaders need to look like? The effective Coach will point out that not everyone has the proclivity for strategic thinking. They will question the possibility that the individual could be successful by playing to her existing strengths.

Another common request for the Coach, presented in various guises, is to coach someone to become more 'emotionally intelligent'. These may be individuals who are seen as lacking self-awareness, socially inept, abrasive or disruptive. This can be a very valuable endeavour for the individual in terms of personal growth and a more effective impact upon an organisation. An effective Coach will recognise the potential benefits of such an assignment but also recognise when she is being asked to help an individual conform to cultural expectations and 'norms' such as: 'we don't rock the boat around here'.

It has been amplified by our work with The GC Index® how important it is for the Coach to challenge, clarify and manage expectations about coaching outcomes. For example, we have seen how obsessive individuals (those we call Game Changers and Polishers) can be disruptive, challenging and not interested in 'social niceties' when they care strongly about something. Helping these individuals to become aware of, and manage, their impact is one thing, asking them to conform in ways that will stifle their talents is another. Andrew Dyckhoff's case study, on page 85, is an example of how to effectively manage such assignments.

Lee Lam's case study is a good example of the way in which The GC Index® can be used, in a coaching context, to manage stakeholder expectations and build upon an individual's strengths at work. Bjorn Kirchdorfer's case study demonstrates the value of recognising an individual's talents and supporting them through complementary relationships.

Case studies from Simon Phillips and Dr John Mervyn-Smith show how The GC Index® can be used to bring focus to the development of an individual's capabilities in a way that helps them to adapt to the demands of their role.

The case studies from Mike O'Dell, Kully Jaswal and Gaylin Jee, describe the value of The GC Index® when it comes to helping people making career transitions: aligning their talents to their ambitions and adapting their approach for success.

As you will see from these case studies in the second half of the book, The GC Index® helps Coaches challenge assumptions of 'what talent looks like' as well as their efforts upon the task:

29

'You have talent, how can we develop it'.

We have selected these case studies to provide you with a variety of practical examples that you may encounter when coaching clients. The focus of the case studies include a range of different scenarios, from using The GC Index® to support career decisions to managing organisational change.

The GC Index®

6

The GC Index®

The GC Index®:
Understanding Game Changers

The GC Index® was born from an increasing need
for organisations to find people who can drive
transformational change through creativity and
innovation. Organisations survive and thrive when
they have the capability to develop, change and
adapt. The life-blood of organisational longevity and
success is: 'Ideas, invention and re-invention'.

> "It is not the strongest of the
> species that survives, nor the
> most intelligent, but the one
> most responsive to change."

Charles Darwin, 1809

The story of Paul Buchheit (2), a Google
engineer in 2001, illustrates the potential
and power of people to make a game-
changing, transformational impact on
organisations. He started using his '20%
time' (the one day a week Google allowed
staff to work on new projects) to develop
a new product. Initially codenamed
Caribou, the product was, after nearly
three years of development, released as
Gmail and would reinvent the entire web-
based email category, capturing 53% of
the market.

Gmail, now one of Google's most successful products, was not an idea formulated by management and developed in a classic top-down 'waterfall' manner. Developing an email product was not even part of Google's corporate strategy at the time. It was one engineer's 'passion project', driven by the belief that email services should be better.

It is an example of how one Game Changer can positively transform the destiny of not just one organisation but an entire industry.

The question though, from London-based business insight and talent consultancy eg.1, was: 'What makes people like Paul Buchheit different, if anything?' eg.1's experience had been that these individuals could not be readily defined using existing capability frameworks, yet they were the very people organisations were increasingly asking them to identify and develop.

33

These requests prompted Nathan Ott and Andrew Gray from eg.1 to commission a research project to explore and, hopefully, answer the following questions:

- Do these individuals who drive transformational change through creativity and innovation – people they called the 'Game Changers' – exist in the corporate world?

- If they do, what characteristics differentiate them from their colleagues?

- Can we assess these characteristics in a meaningful way, a way that can support the identification, recruitment, retention and development of these individuals?

This first phase of our research into the characteristics of Game Changers was carried out in collaboration with Duke University's Corporate Education Journal 'Dialogue'. The results of this study are described in detail in the publication: 'The DNA of a Game Changer'. It can be downloaded from www.thegcindex.com (3).

We collected data from 1:1 interviews with managers and executives using a repertory grid approach to examine the questions noted above. The headline findings were both enlightening and encouraging. More specifically, analyses of the data revealed that:

- Our interviewees readily recognised Game Changers in the world of work.

- Game Changers were working at all levels within organisations and game-changing talent was not seen to be associated exclusively with hierarchical success.

- Game Changers were seen to have characteristics that differentiate them, in a statistically significant way, from colleagues described in our interviews as 'high potentials' and successful senior executives.

Further analyses and reflection upon the characteristics of Game Changers described by our interviewees, suggested that they clustered into two categories:

Imagination

A capacity for original thought: the ability to generate ideas and see possibilities that others do not; to be creative.

Obsession

An obsessive, compulsive nature that compels them to give expression to their creativity and to turn ideas into reality.

You may recognise these qualities in people you know or have worked with, or perhaps, in yourself.

Reading books like James Dyson's 'Against the Odds: An Autobiography' (4) will certainly bring these characteristics to life. Dyson, in an obsessive way, 'pushed the boundaries' and challenged accepted norms, to achieve success. The following quote captures the tenacious persistence that we have come to recognise in obsessive Game Changers.

"You need a stubborn belief in an idea to see it realised."

Giving up was never an option for Dyson – he believed in something and was going to make it happen.

Maxine Clark's story, as mentioned in The Transformative CEO: Impact Lessons from Industry Game Changers (5), also reflects the game-changing ability to see possibilities that others don't. As Founder and CEO of Build-A-Bear Workshop,

35

she followed her dream with passion. She says:

"When a ten-year old girl innocently asked, 'Why can't we make our own teddy bears?', the light bulb flashed. My dream for Build-A-Bear Workshop was born. Every adult I asked about the idea said it would not work."

Therefore 'The DNA of a Game Changer' study helped when it comes to understanding these people we call Game Changers. We distilled some defining characteristics through our research, but the original challenge remained: 'How could we help organisations to identify, recruit, manage and nurture them?'

It was not enough to say that they are imaginative and obsessive people, we wanted to find a more sophisticated way of measuring these qualities.

To help us with this challenge we involved Professor Adrian Furnham. Adrian is one of the world's leading authorities on the assessment of individual differences. His team provided us with a comprehensive review of the literature relevant to the nature of imagination and obsession and this review helped us to prepare a series of questions designed to measure these two constructs. This was the beginning of the development of The GC Index®. The technical underpinnings are described in detail in 'The GC Index® : The Technical Story So Far' which is available via discover@thegcindex.com, on request.

The Emergence of The GC Index®

With a set of questions for reliably
measuring the two key constructs of
imagination and obsession, The GC
Index® model began to take shape.
This process was supported and
accelerated by a number of organisations.
Pascal Viginier, for example, the Group
Chief Information Officer for Orange,
played a pivotal role in developing our
thinking. He and his team encouraged
us to see, within our data, the possibility
for describing significant contributions
to transformational change other than
that of the Game Changer. Clients like
Pascal asked questions of our data in
ways that inspired us to see the world of
organisational talent and transformational
change through their eyes.

Encouragingly, the corporate leaders
we talked to wanted to identify their
Game Changers, but they also wanted
to understand what our data was telling
us about the ways in which others could
make an impact and contribution to a
role, team and organisation. What did
it mean, for example, if someone is
obsessive but not imaginative? How
could these differences come together
as complementary contributions? This
prompted the follow on publication: 'The
DNA of a Game-Changing Team'(6).

An examination of our data, including the
ways in which people responded to the
questions on our initial questionnaire,
revealed five distinct, well-defined ways
in which people make an impact at work.
The culmination of this work was The GC
Index® framework, which is displayed in
the image overleaf.

37

The GC Index® Framework

The GC Index® framework measures and describes five proclivities, five different ways in which people are inclined to make an impact and contribution.

These five proclivities are described in detail later. As you read about the behaviours associated with each proclivity, bear in mind that these behaviours are a product of an individual's assumptions about the world, their values and beliefs, 'internal dialogue' – what people say to themselves about their actions and impact upon the world.

The Psychology of The GC Index®

The following diagram presents the 'psychological building blocks' that create the individual differences described by The GC Index®.

In Appendix 2 (see page 137), we present a more detailed picture of what this could look like for each of the five GC Index® proclivities.

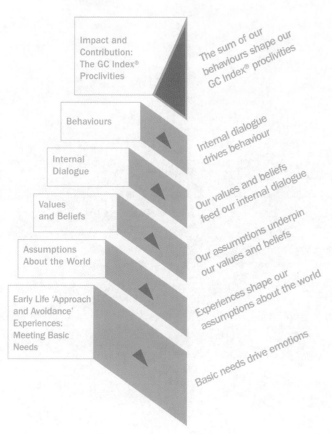

Impact and Contribution: The GC Index® Proclivities

The sum of our behaviours shape our GC Index® proclivities

Behaviours

Internal dialogue drives behaviour

Internal Dialogue

Our values and beliefs feed our internal dialogue

Values and Beliefs

Our assumptions underpin our values and beliefs

Assumptions About the World

Experiences shape our assumptions about the world

Early Life 'Approach and Avoidance' Experiences: Meeting Basic Needs

Basic needs drive emotions

The GC Index® Model of Making an Impact

The GC Index® Proclivities

The Strategist
MAPS THE FUTURE

The Game Changer
TRANSFORMS THE FUTURE

The Play Maker
ORCHESTRATES THE FUTURE

The Implementer
BUILDS THE FUTURE

The Polisher
CREATES A FUTURE TO BE PROUD OF

How are you Making Your Impact?

Read through the descriptions of the five GC Index® proclivities presented over the next few pages. Each is different, all are important. As you read them consider how you are currently making an impact in your team and organisation.

Strategists

At Their Best

Strategists see patterns and trends in events and data. This could be the Chief Marketing Officer who sees patterns and trends in consumer behaviour, the Chief Financial Officer who sees numerical patterns in a set of accounts or the physician who sees a pattern in a set of symptoms. It could be the individual who sees repeated behaviours within a dysfunctional family.

Strategists ask 'why', they look for links between events and data. They seek to 'fit together the pieces of the jigsaw', to 'join up the dots' in a way that helps them to see the 'bigger picture'. At their best they can bring a logical and analytical mind to making predictions about the future based upon the patterns of the past.

As People

Strategists like to make sense of their world. They tend to assume a causality between events that leads them to ask: 'how are these events related?' and to postulate: 'if this, then this.' This approach helps them to bring some structure to their world, to bring, at times, order from apparent chaos or arbitrariness. Making sense of things is often the basis for action; it will bring purpose, energy and focus to action.

As Leaders

Strategists will lead with possibilities
that are a product of what has gone
before. They will present their ideas in a
way that engages others and mobilises
action. They will bring optimism and
energy to a fundamental human need
to predict the future by mastering the
present. Ideas will become strategies
that will become plans of action, and
action will help people to feel potent.

Game Changers

At Their Best

Game Changers, at their best, see possibilities that have the potential to change the landscape of their world. This could be a musician, artist, or writer whose work influences others for generations. It may be the designer or the inventor whose work is original, not derivative, or the amateur chef with original recipes constantly popping into their head.

Game Changers imagine possibilities that others don't, and they engage others with the excitement and the vision of what is possible. Their contribution to the world is one of transformational change rather than incremental change, i.e. they see what might be rather than wanting to improve or change what is.

As People

Game Changers have a need for creative expression. Their creativity coincides with uncensored, seemingly free-associative thinking; they rule things in rather than ruling them out. They allow themselves to imagine, to dream.

They don't feel constrained by a need to build upon what has gone before or by 'tried and tested' ways of doing things. They have a way to imagine how things could be and, when they become obsessed with an idea, how things should be.

Game Changers do not see themselves
as risk takers. For them, a greater
sense of loss and regret will come
from **not** doing something rather
than trying to do something.

Creativity for them is, to some extent,
a manifestation of their identity, of how
they see themselves. Given this, being
free to express themselves is vital to
their sense of well-being.

As Leaders
Game Changers may often be seen as
inflexible, tenacious to the point of being
a 'dog with a bone'. Their single-minded
nature may mean that they are not seen
as open to influence and this will distort
relationships for some.
At their best, they
will lead through
the power of ideas
and possibilities.

GC

Play Makers

At Their Best

Play Makers, at their very best, invest in their relationships at work. Their focus is upon getting things done through the strength of their relationships and through shared endeavour and teamwork. They enable rather than delegate and take pleasure in seeing others shine. They are orchestrators and facilitators who like to get the very best from others. This could be the team captain who knows how to get the best out of everyone, the marketing person who effortlessly pulls everyone together to put on a wonderful event or the practice manager of a Doctor's surgery ensuring everyone contributes in making it run like clockwork.

As People

Play Makers believe that once you get the relationships 'right', then things will naturally follow and will get done. They are instinctive 'people gatherers' who are happy for others to be in the spotlight. At their best, they will know what makes people tick and know how to motivate and influence them. This will often reflect a high degree of emotional intelligence. For Play Makers collective achievement is more important than individual glory.

As Leaders

Play Makers do not seek to dominate, they are quite the opposite from 'command-and-control' leaders. Their approach is to be involving and inclusive, to facilitate and seek consensus. They use the language of 'we' rather than 'I' and, consistent with this, can seem quite understated at times. At their best, they are able see how people can make a contribution to broader objectives.

By definition, Play Makers value the sort of group cohesion that they believe is necessary to drive performance: 'we are all in this together'. Their inclination is to seek harmony in groups although the skilful ones will not shy away from confrontation, they will manage conflict in such a way that it produces cohesion rather than fragmentation.

Implementers

At Their Best

Implementers, at their very best, get things done, they deliver. Their philosophy, and practice, is one of practical, pragmatic problem solving. They will often have a reputation as a 'safe pair of hands', someone who can be relied upon to get things done in a dependable way. They are outcome focused and will get things done without being a slave to the process. In groups and teams, they will bring task-focused energy and urgency. This could be the project manager who needs to deliver outcomes quickly for their client, it could be the tour guide ensuring her guests see as much as they can on her trip or the HR manager who just wants to make things happen.

As People

Implementers are, typically, driven by the satisfaction that comes from tangible achievements. Consistent with this, they will enjoy the challenge of finding ways to do things, finding solutions to practical problems and ways around obstacles. They can be innovative and flexible in the process. Their pragmatism is such that they can accept when an outcome is 'good enough', and 'fit for purpose'.

As Leaders

Effective Implementers, as leaders, are typically, high energy people, action and outcome focused. They will tend to 'lead by example' demonstrating resilience to setbacks. They may tend to rely upon others for ideas and broader strategic direction given that their real strength and, valued contribution, is to make things happen.

Nonetheless, effective Implementers need to be able to articulate the 'why' of action as well as the 'how'. They may also need to manage their frustration with analysis paralysis or abstract notions that don't fit with real, operational needs. Effective Implementers will have developed the skills to help others i.e. Strategists to 'test' ideas and turn them into a reality.

Polishers

At Their Best

Polishers embody the philosophy and practice of continuous improvement. They seek to set the standard for excellence within their role and organisation. They can take products, processes and procedures and constantly seek to improve them.

This could be the receptionist constantly striving to have the perfect welcome for their visitors, the branding consultant ensuring that the new product design is the best as it can be before it goes to print or the gardener striving for the perfect lawn.

As People

Within any effective Polisher is a perfectionist nature. They derive energy and satisfaction from taking solutions and developing them to the point of perfection and excellence, maximising their potential.

They will be able to understand and articulate the commercial, competitive advantage derived from continuous improvement. Consistent with this approach, they will value learning from review: 'what could we do better, differently?'

When it matters most to them, they will struggle to accept 'good enough'. At an

extreme, they are obsessive. Their drive
for continuous improvement and their striving
for excellence will reflect a determined and
tenacious nature. It also reflects optimism,
the view that something could be better.

They will feel most challenged when they have
to make a decision when a task is good enough,
even though they continue to see possibilities
for improvement.

As Leaders
They will balance the challenge of 'we
can do better' with the support of a 'safe
to fail' culture. They will be demanding,
setting high expectations for themselves
and others. This focus on stretching
others will require a sophisticated skill
set to do it well. At best,
they will inspire
people to perform
to their very best,
at worst, their
demanding nature
may inhibit others.
Their drive can
be relentless.

51

The GC Index® with a Focus upon Development

The GC Index® identifies an individual's preferred way to make an impact, a proclivity. This understanding can then be used as a powerful basis for development. For example, someone with a strong Implementer proclivity will be driven to get things done but there may be much that they can learn about managing their workload, setting priorities or organising projects.

Andrew Dyckhoff's and Sammy Rashed's case studies, included in the second half of this book, illustrate this point. Their work demonstrates how The GC Index® can bring awareness to an individual's proclivities in a way that then helps to bring focus to the capabilities needed to develop their proclivities, to make it a strength. This understanding forms the basis for a game-changing equation for getting the very best from people.

The equation is this:

A STRENGTH = PROCLIVITY + CAPABILITIES

In his case study for example (page 85), Andrew describes his work with a valued Game Changer. She had the characteristics of a Game Changer, described on page 85, but was failing to reach her potential in terms of making an impact. With an understanding of the capabilities needed to be an effective Game Changer (see page 86 – The GC Index®: Role Capabilities), Andrew was able to bring a practical and effective focus to their coaching relationship.

The following example will give you a practical idea of this equation in action.

Imagine that you have been asked to coach a Chief Operating Officer. Her profile delivered by The GC Index® reveals an Implementer proclivity.

Her approach is a very pragmatic one, her energy focused upon delivering tangible outcomes. She has little interest in game-changing ideas and does not think like a Strategist.

You explore her role and the contribution she wants to make to the leadership team. This exploration, together with an understanding of how Implementers can complement their colleagues in teams, (Page 86) leads you both to the conclusion that she needs to focus upon developing the following skills:

- Evaluating and reality checking, in a constructive way, the operational feasibility of possibilities generated by Strategist colleagues.

- Helping the leadership team to 'move' from debating ideas and possibilities to making decisions about actions.

- Bringing operational details to strategic objectives.

- Managing her impatience with 'fanciful ideas'.

Can people develop their proclivities?

This then, is an example for how the equation: A Strength = Proclivity + Capabilities can work in practice. That people can develop specific skills is an obvious point. However, our equation also raises the question: 'can people develop their proclivities?' The world of learning and development has been at times, quite bullish on this point over the last few decades with some practitioners taking the view that anything is possible: anyone can become a leader, anyone can be creative and so on. Our work with The GC Index® has prompted us to revisit the notion that people can develop their proclivities; it's an issue that

53

has often been subject of debate and discussion.

Our experience of using The GC Index® in a coaching setting supports an optimistic view that human beings are adaptable to some extent. The case studies presented

Think differen

by Mike O'Dell and Simon Phillips support the notion that people can, relative to the proclivities outlined in the framework, adapt when they need to. People can take on the role of Implementer, for example, when things need to be done and they are the only ones who can do it.

Our work with individuals also suggests that people new into their careers typically need to 'win their spurs' by 'doing', delivering in a task-focused way. Few people will be paid in the early years of their careers for being Strategists or Play Makers.

However, we also see, limits to adaptability that reflect both what an individual is capable of and what they have energy for. Take for example, the Director in a consulting firm who agreed with his Strategist profile but who was working on a long-term 'due diligence' project that required a rigorous attention to detail an ideal task for a Polisher. He was able to do the task, to adapt, but he found the work draining. It was taking more energy than it was giving, and he felt increasingly depleted. He was thinking of leaving the job.

Our conversations with people about their Game Changer proclivity also supports the view that human adaptability can be limited. People invariably agree with the Game Changer aspect of their profile.

The high scoring Game Changers typically describe seeing possibilities that others don't and of doing 'game-changing' things. Those with low scores for this proclivity recognise, usually with some comfort, that they are not creative. There may be skills that people can apply to 'creative problem solving' but this problem-centered creativity is quite different from the possibility-centered creativity that Game Changers demonstrate coupled with their drive for creative expression.

This point was illustrated perfectly in the Apple Think Different Advertisement Campaign where they talk about "...the crazy ones, the misfits and the troublemakers..." They talk about the fact the people who are 'crazy' enough to think they will change the world, are the ones who do.

The effective Coach then, needs to make a considered view when working with their Coachee about the realistic possibilities for development and change. They must take account of the adaptability of human nature in a way that helps an individual manage their 'weaknesses' and 'play to their strengths'. The previous story of the Implementer learning how to make a contribution to the strategic debate, rather than learning how to be a strategic thinker is a good example of this.

The GC Index® along with its Role Capability Framework (Appendix 1) can bring a practical focus to this exploration in a way that helps to shape realistic expectations.

55

The GC Index® and Complementary Relationships at Work

The GC Index® describes five related proclivities. They are related by the core constructs from which they developed, namely, Imagination and Obsession. Given this, it's not surprising that, in practice, the proclivities complement each other.

This complementarity is a theme in Bjorn and Gaylin's case studies. Their examples illustrate an obvious point: it's so much easier for people to collaborate when they understand what they bring to a relationship – how they complement others, and what they need from a relationship. Collaboration, after all, is sustained by the reciprocity of 'giving and getting' and The GC Index® framework is a readily accessible language for thinking about the nature of the exchange that provides the basis for a productive relationship.

Collaboration is defined as: The action of working with someone to produce something.

The GC Index® would argue that having two Implementers working together might be

Which one is collaboration?

We're making progress, keep pedalling

I think these would help

collaboration by this definition but it may not
necessarily produce the best outcome. The GC
Index® framework invites us to consider collaboration
as the potential for complementary impact.

Mike Ksenyak, HR Lead at Water For People says,

"The GC Index® is giving our
employees a language to better
discuss leadership, impact and
collaboration. This methodology
is improving the way we work
and will contribute to Water For
People achieving our mission
around the world."

The Beatles is a good example of the power
of complementary proclivities coming together.

Few would deny that Lennon and McCartney
were musical Game Changers. They changed the
landscape of popular music in the early 1960s in
the UK. They transformed the future of music with
many other musicians seeking to imitate them
or offer alternatives. In The Independent's list
of most covered popular songs (5th December
2008), The Beatles feature four times in the
top 10, including first and second.

However, Lennon and McCartney's musical talent
needed to be brought to life and The Beatles did this.
They transformed lyrics and music into the songs
that still influence people today. Collectively, they
were the Implementers and Polishers of creativity.

The Beatles creativity may have lost focus though,
without the talent of Brian Epstein, The Beatles'
manager. He saw, as Strategists do, the bigger
picture. He saw the contribution that they could make

57

to the world of music at the time. He mapped the future. He also took on the role of Play Maker by bringing some cohesion to action when times were difficult, making sure that everyone worked together to achieve shared goals.

Human beings seem to be hard-wired when it comes to appreciating and being drawn to beauty and perfection even when we don't fully understand it. This was the role of George Martin, The Beatles' record producer. He brought his Polisher inclinations to the fore, by perfecting their performances.

The broader point here is captured in the diagram on page 59.

The notion that transformational change is the product of one heroic individual seems seductive, at least in the western world, and consistent with the beginnings of our journey: the quest to find individuals who can drive transformational change.

However, this notion doesn't 'map onto' most people's reality: rarely, if ever, is transformational change in the corporate world, the result of one individual's efforts, even Paul Buchheit's (see page 32).

The myth of the Hero Innovator

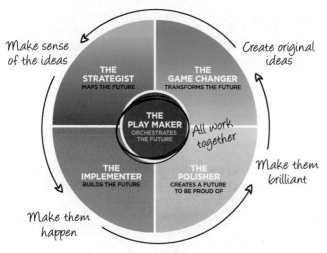

Make sense of the ideas

Create original ideas

THE STRATEGIST
MAPS THE FUTURE

THE GAME CHANGER
TRANSFORMS THE FUTURE

THE PLAY MAKER
ORCHESTRATES THE FUTURE

All work together

THE IMPLEMENTER
BUILDS THE FUTURE

THE POLISHER
CREATES A FUTURE TO BE PROUD OF

Make them brilliant

Make them happen

Experience suggests that innovation and creativity, is the product of the collective efforts of a team.

Telefonica's Alpha project reinforces this point: their game-changing creativity would amount to little without the Strategist's ability to evaluate possibilities within a commercial context and the Implementer and Polisher drive to turn them into a reality.

One test of any framework is how it resonates with people, how well it 'maps onto' their experience of the world and in a way that helps them to act and to turn insights into a practical reality. The GC Index® has been very encouraging in this regard. With a rudimentary understanding of the framework and their own profile, people, when asked, can usually give a practical account of how they can support, complement and collaborate with colleagues at work.

The GC Index® and Multi-Dimensional Leadership

A growing database of GC Index® profiles allowed us to do further research and analyses in 2016. One enquiry led to a multi-dimensional view of leadership. This understanding has key implications for making an impact in the 21st Century.

For many decades, the corporate world has been seduced by the notion that we can produce a definitive list of the personal qualities and characteristics of the successful leader. Much has been written on the subject, often influenced by our understanding of what military leaders look like.

It doesn't take much to dispel this seemingly compelling myth. We often ask corporate leaders to come up with their list of the qualities that they consider define successful leaders and then share them in a group. Invariably, three things happen:

1 . The list goes on forever.

2. People begin to challenge the list and dispute others' views.

3. They always manage to think of successful leaders who do not conform to any or all of the qualities generated.

In 1969, Paul Hersey and Ken Blanchard **(7)** shifted the focus away from personality in our understanding of leadership. They proposed that effective leadership was an interaction between leadership behaviours and the needs of the situation, specifically, the individual(s) being led.

More recent research failed to support the basic premises suggested by their model of 'Situational Leadership' (Fernandez and Vecchio (1997) **(8)**. Nonetheless, it was game–changing work at the time and set the tone for research to come. It tapped into what seems obvious to most of us now, namely that a one-dimensional view of leadership does not fit with our experience of the world: different situations require different styles of leadership.

We can also thank game-changing researchers like Warren Bennis and Bert Nanus **(9)** (Leaders: The Strategies for Taking Charge 1985) who also shifted our focus onto leadership behaviours as a way to understand leadership.

In an elegant and compelling way, they offered us new and practical insights into leadership behaviour. They created a picture of what successful corporate leaders do, not what they are like. Whilst it is possible to challenge their research methodology, importantly, they encouraged a new way of thinking about corporate leadership.

They captured leadership behaviours in what they called the 'Four Strategies':

Strategy 1:

Attention Through Vision – articulating a compelling picture of the future.

Strategy 2:

Meaning Through Communication – creating community and endeavour through communicating a shared purposed.

Strategy 3:

Trust Through Positioning – here is a leader who is going to do what they say they're going to do.

Strategy 4:

The Deployment of Self Through Positive Self Regard – encouraging learning and resourcefulness.

A leadership development assignment carried out by Dr John Mervyn-Smith, in Hong Kong, reinforced the view that these approaches to leadership are also shaped by the demands of the situation.

The client was a transport company that was undergoing radical, transformational, change in one part of the organisation and 'business as usual' in another. In that part of the business going through transformational change, people wanted their leaders to deliver Strategies 1 and 4: 'tell us what we are aiming to achieve and give us the resources/learning to achieve it'. For the business in a stable state, the message to the business leaders was: 'we want you to build a trusting and cohesive community'.

This notion that effective leadership is a product of the 'fit' between the demands of the situation

61

and the leadership style, has been reinforced,
and developed, by our work with The GC Index®.

Two years on from our initial research, our
database revealed the following insights:

- The GC Index® profiles for people feeling engaged
  by and comfortable in their roles are typically
  characterised by two 'dominant' proclivities.

- These two dominant proclivities shape
  the individual's approach to leadership
  and management.

- Two dominant proclivities from five, produces ten
  possible leadership styles. These are presented
  in the diagram on page 63.

- Most importantly, our data reveals that all of
  these combinations are represented by successful
  executives. In other words, it is possible to be a
  successful leader in corporate life with a range
  of leadership styles.

The GC Index® therefore, gives us a framework
for thinking about the diversity of leadership styles.
It also challenges the notion that leadership can
only be defined by one set of capabilities. This multi-
dimensional leadership model is transforming the way
organisations approach leadership development and
assessment.

The GC Index® Multi-Dimensional Leadership

Contemporary Leader

Creative Leader

Visionary Leader

Leader as Coach

Pragmatic Leader

Inspirational Leader

Charismatic Leader

Leader by Example

Inventive Leader

Aspirational Leader

Consider the 20 leaders below and match them to The GC Index Profile® – as you see it of course, there are no definitive answers as they haven't completed The GC Index®.

Think about them in terms of their reputations for driving tangible change (Implementers), building inclusive communities (Play Makers), original thinking (Game Changers), seeing the patterns and trends in their world (Strategists) and obsessive persistence (Polishers).

You can take a look at our conclusions in Appendix 3.

First Row – Left to right: Elon Musk, Michelle Mone, Jack Ma, Jacqueline Gold, Jeff Bezos
Second Row – Left to right: Arianna Huffington, Lakshmi MIttal, Cher Wang, Jo Malone, Ghandi
Third Row – Left to right: JK Rowling, Richard Branson, Henry Ford, Anita Roddick, Martha Lane Fox
Fourth Row – Left to right: Scott Harrison, James Dyson, Oprah Winfrey, Warren Buffett, Beyonce Knowles

The Impactful Coach: Coaching with The GC Index®

7

The Chemistry Meeting

A coaching relationship often starts with a 'chemistry meeting'. It is designed to give the Coachee a sense of choice; it allows them to feel empowered about their own development. However, the actual process often lacks clarity and, as the notion of 'chemistry' suggests, implies a degree of instinct, intuition or 'magic' when it comes to making a decision about whether and how to proceed.

A lack of clarity at this 'Chemistry Meeting' stage can easily lead to muddled or distorted expectations of the coaching process and desired outcomes and then, at some stage, disappointment.

Successful Coaches understand their strengths. They know 'who they are', what their approach is and, therefore, who they can, and cannot help. They have the skills to clarify expectations during initial meetings and the courage to say when they feel that they cannot help. It does take courage as it's never easy to say 'no' to someone who is asking for help.

The GC Index® not only helps a Coach to understand their Coachee, as you will see from the case studies to follow, but it helps a Coach to understand their own approach, to know when they are at their best and, therefore, who they can and cannot help. It's a framework for thinking about the degree of 'fit' between Coach and Coachee that goes beyond alchemy.

Coaching Styles and The GC Index®

What we do know is that, at any point in time, a Coach, when working with their Coachee, will 'sit' somewhere on the 'directive to non-directive' continuum.

- Some will, consistently, be more inclined to be directive: framing problems and issues and offering solutions.

- Some will be more inclined to be non-directive, facilitating the conversation in a way that allows the Coachee to both understand a problem/issue for themselves and define solutions.

- Some will, of course, flex their approach to suit the needs of their Coachee.

All effective Coaches find a balance between being directive and non-directive, not just from Coachee to Coachee but from coaching session to coaching session.

As Coaches, our approach in this regard will reflect our proclivities. We will 'see' things that our Coachee may not appear to. The question then is: 'what do we do with what we see?' What is important is that, as Coaches, we know when and why we are being directive or non-directive with what we see, and that we make conscious decisions that are in the best interests of our Coachee. Without this consciousness, a Coach's behaviour can be driven by their own needs to feel potent, rather than the needs of their client.

The GC Index® Coaching Styles

What is your coaching preference?

Coaches see themselves as helpers and as a consequence, the coaching relationship can be both incredibly rewarding and incredibly challenging. How they help, in terms of style and approach, will vary.

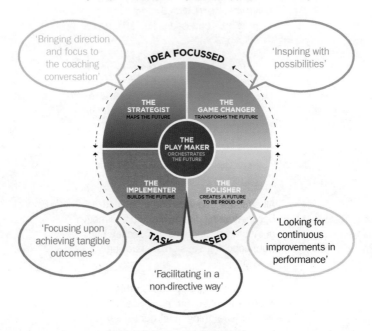

The Play Maker Coach – Facilitates…

The Play Maker approach to coaching is one of facilitating and empowering, more akin to the non-directive counselling approach often associated with therapists like Carl Rogers (10). Their style is not to impose a view but, through listening, summarising and reflecting, to help their Coachee to become more aware and gain insights that lead to meaningful change. Typically, they do not believe that giving or imposing a view is helpful.

The Strategist Coach – Looks for the patterns and trends in their Coachee's life and career…

At their best, the Strategist Coach will help their Coachee to review past events in a way that helps them to learn, adapt and adjust to present and future demands. They will reflect the patterns and themes that they see in a way that helps their Coachee to understand and define actions for themselves. They may take the view that they can 'see' things that, at times, their Coachee cannot.

The Implementer Coach – Focuses upon the practicalities of life and work…

The Implementer Coach will draw upon their experience of the world of work to help their Coachee to focus upon what will help them to meet current goals. They will see the 'how' when it comes to getting things done. They will bring pragmatism and common sense to this pursuit. The Coachee can expect the coaching programme to be defined by agreed aims and a practical focus upon achieving tangible objectives.

The Game Changer Coach – Encourages their Coachee to 'dream' of what is possible rather than dwell on the way things are…

The Game Changer Coach will help people who want to transform their lives: to pursue the career that they always wanted, to be bold, and to take risks in pursuit of their aspirations and dreams. They may articulate possibilities that their Coachee can't or doesn't allow themselves to see.

**The Polisher Coach – Looks for areas
of incremental improvement…**

> Not surprisingly, we often see Polisher Coaches
> in the world of sport. The focus is upon tangible
> but incremental changes that if taken together,
> can have a big impact. The individual who
> wants to develop a particular skill, such as their
> presentation skills, may do well to choose a
> Polisher Coach who will set high standards for
> performance.

Matching the Coach to the Coachee using this
framework can provide great benefits, bringing
focused and productive energy to the coaching
relationship.

Consider the individual who wants help to focus on
the skills needed to manage their boss. They would
fare better with an Implementer Coach who would
bring a pragmatic approach to developing the skills
they need to manage their relationship with their
boss.

The individuals who want to reflect upon why they find
certain people difficult at work, including their boss,
may value the approach of the Play Maker Coach.
Their quest, in the first instance, is for insights that
may, or may not, lead to actions. The Play Maker
Coach will listen, reflect, question and summarise in
a way that facilitates these insights.

The Coaching Contract

In order to get the best from the coaching
relationship, a clear coaching contract at
the outset is essential. This creates clarity
of expectations and brings focus to the
endeavour. This is not to say that things
won't change, and that the focus may
shift, but the coaching contract can take
this into account.

For example, you may be working with a CEO who wants her Coach to be an 'insightful sounding board' helping her to review issues and events and how she manages them as they arise. This expectation brings clarity to your role, and an agreed approach to working together, which can be reviewed over time. A Play Maker Coach who understands the demands on a CEO would be a good fit for this sort of assignment.

This is a very different assignment from the Director who is being 'groomed' for partnership within a consulting firm. The Coachee, existing Partners and the commissioner for the assignment (usually HR), will all have views about what changes they can expect to see over time. Their expectations need to be understood, agreed and managed in a way that can bring a clear focus to coaching conversations. A Strategist Coach who has seen what's needed to make these successful transitions may be a good fit for someone looking to make promotion to Partner.

Coaching raises all sorts of expectations and, from the outset, the Coach's task is to try and make these expectations as explicit as possible. Problems will arise when stakeholders' expectations are unclear or not aligned. It is a rare occasion when coaching can be seen as a 'black box' process in which only the expectations of the Coachee need to be clarified and managed.

The GC Index®, as a framework and language, can help to bring focus and clarity to Coachee and stakeholder expectations. It can be especially useful when stakeholders' expectations are unrealistic and need to be challenged.

As Coaches we often need to give an informed view on whether or not expectations for development are realistic but doing so isn't always easy when the prevailing zeitgeist is that anything can be developed. A Coach has to feel very confident in their judgement or else they are at risk of colluding with unrealistic aims.

71

Take, for example, the talented young manager in a multinational technology company. He had been tagged as 'high potential' and his managers wanted to prepare him for a bigger role that required managing a large team of technologists. His boss saw him as capable, conscientious, likeable and emotionally intelligent. His profile, as displayed by The GC Index®, was that of a Game Changer/Implementer and, consistent with this profile, he was a 'creative, practical problem solver'. However, his Play Maker profile was relatively low. While he was very socially skilled, he had no interest in managing people, as he put it: "I don't do needy". However, he didn't have the courage to say this to his boss.

His profile proved useful in a conversation with his boss. He was able to talk about what engaged and energised him: creative problem solving, and what didn't: managing people. His boss was also a problem solver and, because she valued his talents, she shaped a role that made the most of his talents.

In closing, a coaching contract defines an approach to working together along with a set of achievable and agreed objectives that can be shared, where appropriate, with other stakeholders within the organisation. It provides clear goals, a constant reference point and a focus for conversations. This is the foundation upon which real progress can be built.

As you will see from the following case studies written by a selection of experienced Coaches accredited in The GC Index® around the world (we call them GCologists). The GC Index® framework and language plays an important part in getting the coaching contract right. It brings focus to help Coaches quickly understand their clients and it is this that often improves outcomes and accelerates impact.

Coaching with The GC Index® – Case Studies

Coaches can play a unique role in helping their clients to make a successful impact at work.

With the following case studies, we focus upon how the successful Coach can use The GC Index® to:

- Maximise their impact in their current role.

- Recognise, play to, and build upon, strengths.

- Define and develop those capabilities needed to succeed in aspirational roles.

- Manage key stakeholder expectations when it comes to contribution and ambitions.

- Open their minds to what's possible.

Case Study Contents

Coaching with The GC Index® – Case Studies

Each person who takes The GC Index® will receive a score of 1-10 for each of The GC Index® roles.

A Role Score of 1-3
A proclivity score of 1 to 3 suggests little energy or inclination for the role. The individual may tend to avoid roles of this sort when they can. As a consequence, they may not have developed the requisite skills to perform well in these roles.

A Role Score of 4-6
A proclivity score of 4 to 6 suggests that the individual may have some energy and inclination for this role but not predominantly so. If and when they take on these roles, success is likely to be more dependent upon discipline than the inherent satisfaction they may derive from the role. Other roles may engage then more readily.

A Role Score of 7-10
A proclivity score of 7 to 10 suggests that an individual's natural energy and inclination is to take on this role. Their ability to be effective within the role will depend upon experience and the degree to which they have had opportunities to develop role-related skills.

KEY:

Strategist | Game Changer | Play Maker | Implementer | Polisher

1. From Outlier to Centre of Action

Coach: Sammy Rashed,
Principal at SRCD
and Co-Founder of
The Beyond Group

Coaching Context
As part of our organisational
transformation work we
often provide coaching
to developing leaders.
In one such case I was
coaching a female leader,
Ilse, who had recently been hired by a large multinational company at its headquarters in Switzerland.
Her role was to help develop a global function's
strategy and prepare its transformation. She was
recruited for, and initially highly regarded for, her
direct approach, creativity and ability to see many
paths towards achieving goals.

Ilse had been hired with the encouraging message:
'please help us change'. But this was quickly
replaced with 'you are standing out too much
and need to fit in fast!'

Within the first year of being hired we began to see
stress develop between my Coachee and her boss.
These tensions eventually resulted in a shift of her
coaching programme from executive development
to remediation.

Luckily, this occurred at a time when we had
carried out an extensive search for diagnostic
tools that would support our coaching regimen.
We opted to use The GC Index® as a way to
understand the match between individuals and
teams for accomplishing their assigned missions.

Coaching Objectives

The message from our Coachee's boss, the global function head, about our Coachee was: 'You stand out too much and need to fit in more.' The expectation of the business then, was of a 'cultural reintegration programme' – while this was possible it simply 'felt wrong'.

From our assessment, it was clear that what emerged as a fundamental cultural mismatch was eventually going to prove to be unrewarding for both parties. The coaching focus became one of helping her to manage her exit and find a role within which she could thrive.

Coaching Themes

Within this focus for our coaching conversations, Ilse wanted to understand the nature of the mismatch in order to gain insights into why it had been so stressful and distressing and to learn how to avoid such a mismatch in the future.

In order to help our Coachee gain these insights, she completed The GC Index®. Her profile displayed below provided her with what she described as an 'aha' moment producing an unprecedented clarity about her impact upon others.

Moreover, she realised that her style and the impact that went with it was not suited to her current role or organisation.

You will see from her profile below that she is someone with a strong Game Changer proclivity, someone with a strong need for creative expression and, with it, a need to bring new ideas and possibilities, to challenge the 'status quo'. While the business valued these qualities and believed they needed someone like this,

77

the reality was that they were not ready for them and couldn't accommodate them. She was seen as too disruptive, too threatening. An accommodation on her part, fitting in, would have meant that she would have had to stifle her talent.

These insights also helped her to take a considered view about the sort of organisational culture within which she would thrive, an understanding that would form the basis for her next career decision.

Coaching Outcomes

The life changing impact of this coaching programme, supported by The GC Index®, was that the Coachee fully recognised that her preferred style of operating (with a strong Game Changer influence) was sadly at odds with a company that had a long history of being very conservative and hugely risk averse.

Ilse had begun to question what was wrong with her. But The GC Index® profile highlighted her strengths, helping her understand her own drive for success and realise that there are many other successful people like her.

The insights from The GC Index® profile also gave her a successful target profile for the type of organisations she wanted to focus on in her job search.

She resigned from the company, which was the right decision, and pursued a new career with a company that really does value Game Changers and whose needs more closely matched her preferred work style.

The job search wasn't easy and, at times, a little discouraging, but by helping her build a clear vision of what type of organisation would be a 'good fit' for her, she persisted and hasn't 'looked back' since. Within a few months of looking she landed a role as VP Transformation in a global organisation looking to turn around the function.

Sammy said:

"The GC Index® profiling is a great tool to 'have in the box'. It gives individuals a concrete basis for understanding how they work and often this can help in understanding why a person is particularly successful in one environment but not another. In particular, as a Coach, we often have a 'feeling' about an individual but can't quite put our finger on that quality that is either helping or hindering them. The GC Index® helps us understand our coachees better so we can be more useful to them."

Sammy's Biography
Helping organisations and individuals strategise, crystallise, and realise their unique contribution, Sammy's experience spans 25 years in project management, productivity, strategy, and personal development.

 www.beyondgrp.com

2. Head of HR to Entrepreneur

Coach: Kully Jaswal
Executive Coach
and Principal at
Next Step Partners

Coaching Context
Jasmine had spent
her career working in a
number of in-house HR
roles. When the coaching
began, she was the Head
of HR for a large law firm
in Asia, leading a team of 15 people. Feeling ready
and seeking to explore other career options she
sought my support.

Coaching Objectives
Jasmine had over 15 years of
experience working in HR related
roles and, while she was extremely
successful in her career, she wasn't
feeling challenged and wanted to focus
on building her coaching and leadership
skills.

She took the view that she would find
greater career satisfaction if she were
to align her personal strengths, values
and skills with her 'ideal' role. This
was to be, in broad terms, the focus for
the coaching relationship; defining and
making a transition to her ideal role.

Coaching Themes
One of Jasmine's core values was independence
and she had always wanted to start her own
business. So, one of her key objectives for the
12-month coaching programme was to explore

81

this as an option and decide if starting her own company would be a good choice. And, if so, to create a clear plan as to how to do it.

As part of our preliminary explorations, Jasmine completed The GC Index®. One of the 'aha' moments from her profile report delivered by The GC Index® (see profile below) were her lower scores for the proclivities of Implementer and Polisher. She realised that without a team, and the right people to support her, she would struggle with routine detail and implementation. While she may have good ideas as a Strategist, there is a danger that she may never make them happen.

During the coaching sessions, I shared the book 'Art of Possible' (11) by Kate Tojeiro as a suggested read because it was written by a fellow GCologist with a similar profile. The book focuses on re-framing thoughts and ideas of what is possible.

She realised that she felt most energised when creating a strategy (Strategist), generating ideas (Game Changer) and collaborating with people (Play Maker). With this in mind, she began to explore the idea of starting a business with other people.

She found an ideal business partner who had already done some of the groundwork and was more focused on some of the details. She recognised that they had complementary proclivities. After spending a few months creating a business plan that she was excited about, this quickly turned into an ideal business partnership.

Coaching Outcomes

Jasmine left her high profile corporate role and started a new and exciting life as an entrepreneur in February 2018, she is now helping to build a start-up: Talent Management and HR Consulting firm, Ka-Bloom Group.

Her role is to focus on building up the business, initially in Hong Kong, focusing on impactful talent solutions for both individuals and organisations. She will be 'playing to her strengths' of helping clients to develop business strategies. She will also continue to focus upon building her coaching practice.

Coaching sessions continue, and focus on helping her to make an effective transition into her new role.

Jasmine said:

"The insights from The GC Index® were an excellent way for me to think about the kind of leadership role my strengths and inclinations play to. Taking these insights on my strengths, and areas for development, into the design of my next steps has helped me work towards a new opportunity that I feel removes some of the doubts I had about the change."

Kully said:

"The GC Index® is an excellent tool for coaches to understand our clients' strengths, potential, and development areas, highlighting areas to focus on for a new role/career. The GC Index® profile reports are insightful, helping clients to realise how they can make a game-changing impact in any organisation or role!"

Kully's Biography

Kully brings to her work 15 years of business experience in London and across Europe specialising in risk management and operational reviews. Kully was a Director for Deloitte UK and worked with a variety of clients and projects in multiple sectors.

 www.nextsteppartners.com

3. Navigating the Future

Coach: Andrew Dyckhoff, Director and Business Mentor at Merryck & Co

Coaching Context
Lee was in a senior marketing role in China for a leading global brand of sportswear. She was unhappy and frustrated by her role and the organisation. She didn't feel listened to when it came to those things that were obvious to her and that she felt passionate about.

Coaching Objectives
Our coaching relationship was, in the context of the organisation, preparing her for a new role. Lee was not sure whether she would stay with the organisation and, given her level of frustration, felt that she needed to make a decision one way or another. In broad terms then, the coaching objective was to help her to reach a considered decision and determine what her next career move should be.

Coaching Themes
I asked Lee to complete The GC Index® as a means of understanding her proclivities and motivations.

Her profile is presented below. It shows, consistent with her frustrations, a very strong Game Changer inclination coupled with a strong Polisher drive. As Game Changers do, she has many ideas and sees

85

lots of possibilities in the world around her. She is also hugely driven to make her ideas happen and to turn ideas into a reality. However, she faced the challenge, so typical of many strong Game Changers, of communicating her ideas to others, having them see what she sees as clearly as she sees it.

As Polishers can be, she was uncompromising in her high standards and focused on delivering the outcomes. She had little time or interest for investing in relationships and the challenge of organisational influence, of engaging 'hearts and minds'.

Receiving her profile and feedback was a revelation for her. Immediately she understood why she was seen as different, rather than just 'feeling' different. The profile helped her recognise that she needed to learn how to communicate or re-frame her ideas in a way that the Strategists and Implementers could understand.

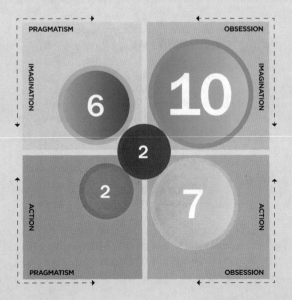

Coaching Outcomes

Lee is a very intelligent and capable individual. With these insights about her approach and her impact she was quickly able to develop a sophisticated approach to engaging, influencing and persuading. She developed skills and patience for helping others to see the world the way that she did.

She was quickly promoted to run a $1 billion part of the regional business and has since been promoted again to run the global brand ambassador network.

Lee said:

"I have learned to channel my non-linear thinking into a linear way of communication to then inspire and communicate my thoughts to a broader group of people."

Andrew said:

"The GC Index® is like the one piece in a Chinese puzzle that puts everything together. When I as an individual understand how I contribute to my organisation and how this fits with others' contributions, we can collectively become effective in driving innovation. We do this by ensuring that we have people who: have the ideas; who turn them into a plan; who build it; who continuously make it better and people who help us work together."

Andrew's Biography

Andrew has had a variety of roles from CEO to administrative, finance, marketing, and front line sales with experience in working with different cultures. He believes in helping leaders understand who they uniquely are in the world, at work and at home.

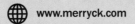 www.merryck.com

4. The Challenge of Leading Change in the Health Sector

Coach: Simon Phillips,
Founder of The Change
Maker Group

Coaching Context
The UK's NHS is
constantly changing.
Sarah, my Coachee, has
experienced, and survived,
no less than six major
organisational changes
in her career!

When she asked me to Coach her, she was leading
a whole organisation of 140 people through a
programme of change. To that point her experience
has been limited to supporting a small team of five
to ten.

Not only was the scale of the change complex
but Sarah also had multiple stakeholder groups
to manage, including an executive team that was
struggling to work cohesively and collaboratively.

Coaching Objectives
The leadership challenge for Sarah was
to transform the performance of the
executive team while, simultaneously,
driving complex strategic organisational
change.

Sarah's profile, delivered by The GC
Index® and presented below, reflects an
approach to leadership that had made
her successful. More specifically, she
had achieved success through aligning

89

action to strategic objectives (Strategist) and bringing energy and urgency to delivering tangible outcomes (Implementer). It was a directive approach that she knew she would need to 'flex' to be successful in her current role.

She recognised that she needed to get things done through persuasion and influence; she didn't have the formal authority to 'tell people what to do'. She needed, then, to develop her skills as a Play Maker and this was the focus of our coaching conversations.

Coaching Themes

Sarah recognised her leadership approach reflected in The GC Index® profile, as shown below. As a Strategist, she saw the patterns and trends of change within the NHS; she was able to 'see the bigger picture'. Supported by years of NHS experience, she trusted her judgement. As an Implementer, she had built a reputation for driving change and 'getting things done'. With clear objectives she would bring energy and drive to getting things done.

Her Game Changer profile also reflects her alertness to new ideas and possibilities, a valuable quality in someone responsible for driving change.

However, Sarah realised that she needed to change her approach to effectively manage the subtleties of organisational politics within a complex stakeholder landscape. She needed to be able to 'engage hearts and minds' in the process of 'taking people with her' on the journey of change.

The GC Index® framework gave Sarah an uncomplicated way of thinking about her approach to leadership and ability to crystallise, in her mind, the skills and behaviours associated with being a Play Maker. These included being inclusive, building consensus, managing concerns and anxieties about change, involving people in defining problems as well as solutions.

Our initial focus was upon building her team; making it 'fizz'. It was a very action-focussed team of strong Implementers, but there was no strategic clarity – 'what are we trying to achieve collectively?' The absence of a clear strategy meant there was little leverage to bring people together and the risk of working in 'silos'.

As a strong Strategist, Sarah could have stepped into this leadership vacuum and presented the strategy to the team. However, she needed to role model a collaborative, consensus-seeking approach that her team would need, individually and collectively, to take with their stakeholders.

To bring the team together, she worked on thinking and behaving like a Play Maker and this became her key focus. How could they orchestrate collaboration? How could they stimulate greater, and committed, alignment across functions in a way that supported the broader goals of the NHS in their region?

Coaching Outcomes

The complexity of the NHS environment has not changed. If anything, it is becoming even more difficult to discern where the organisation is 'going to land'. However, the dynamic in Sarah's team has greatly improved.

She has encouraged her team, as senior leaders, to think strategically, and they now have a desire to understand how 'everything fits together', how their actions can contribute to broader goals in a collective way. By focussing themselves on the 'what', they were able to challenge their own thinking when it came to the 'how' of getting things done.

Sarah said:

"The GC Index® helped us get down to business much quicker than I expected. In turn, this increased our confidence in the tool and we're now using it to rebalance our Governing Body and reorganise our core activities; making them more strengths focused."

Simon said:

"Without The GC Index®, this programme could have easily become all about personalities. Instead, my Coachee and her team spotted the gaps in strengths that were inhibiting performance and got busy fixing them."

Simon's Biography
Simon is an inspirational Change Maker, specialising in the people side of business improvement. His purpose is to 'Create a Million Change Makers.' Covering the full organisational development spectrum from organisational design through to development, he is also a passionate professional development specialist and Coach.

 www.thechangemakergroup.com

93

5. Challenging Team Dynamics and Performance

Coach: Angie Beeston, Business Coach, Mentor, Trainer and Facilitator. MD of Evolution 4 Business

Coaching Context
My client, James, had been in his role with a global organisation for two years. In that time, he had experienced many changes in management, ownership and industry demands.

He had previously worked in a number of HR roles, at middle management level, in other companies. When I was asked to coach him he had been promoted to a senior management role.

He was part of a team of ten people and the organisation was on the verge of going through more change. Due to the difficulties of the dynamics in the team, the impending change was causing issues with engagement, motivation and performance.

Coaching Objectives
James needed to understand how to de-escalate the potential stresses and pressures, not just for himself but for the whole team and, while doing so, maintain a high level of service for both internal and external stakeholders in the business.

Employee engagement sits at the heart

of their business and, therefore, understanding leadership styles was imperative to help implement successful strategic change.

James' profile, delivered by The GC Index® (see below), shows that his approach is based upon being an Implementer. This had enabled him to get things done with energy and urgency, which is just perfect for a role in HR, where completing and finishing tasks is vital, and to tight deadlines.

James' Polisher inclination had also helped to support the demands made upon a busy, dynamic HR team. He focused on getting things done to a high standard when he needed to.

With a leadership style of Leader by Example (combined Implementer and Polisher), James knew he could bring much to the team to help get things done. But he was also very aware he would need to be more flexible, and adapt to change in order to encourage individuals, and the whole team, to do the same.

He realised there would need to be more of a Play Maker in his approach to enable the team to be comfortable and happy with change.

One of the key issues within the team was a slight conflict of personalities, which was causing friction between James and two others. He recognised, as the senior manager, that he needed to understand and appreciate the different ways team memebrs look at things and strengths they bring.

Coaching Themes
The GC Index® profile, as shown below, helped James to understand and confirm his strongest areas of leadership style, yet give a clear picture of those gaps for his own development.

As an Implementer, James was very good at getting things done and had a reputation for being reliable and bringing energy and focus to delivering operational objectives.

This Implementer style of fixing things, combined with his Polisher skills, had served him well.

James' profile suggested his leadership approach was more task focused and ' hands-on'. He was acutely aware that this might have been part of the reason for the conflict with the two team members. In this more senior role, he had to become more strategic and step out of the day-to-day, trusting his team to undertake the operational responsibilities.

With a lower Game Changer score, James became aware that sometimes he was too focused on the 'tried and tested' and needed to be more future conscious, willing to try new areas. Certainly, James needed to develop the key skill, with the impending change in the business, of being more open to new ideas and possibilities.

James realised he had to flex his leadership approach to be able to manage his team much better and enable them to feel more engaged.

He was keen to strive to become more Leader as Coach, which meant he needed to develop as a Play Maker. Being a Leader as Coach would enable him to help his team to see what was possible and to realise their potential.

He would need to be more 'hands-off' where appropriate and give others the freedom to perform and to 'shine'. He was keen to help support the whole team, and wider company, to engage in this new approach and this became our key focus during the coaching – how to get the team to step up, be allowed to undertake key tasks (with some guidance). More importantly, the aim was to reduce the pressure and stress that James had previously been under due to this very task focused, hands-on approach.

Coaching Outcomes

James was open to change and had a strong commitment to making progress. These qualities underpinned possitive changes in his approach to leadership and the dynamics and performance of his team.

The conflict has been resolved and one of the two individuals involved now has a much better relationship with her colleagues and James. Interestingly the other individual decided to move on as the leadership fit and new team approach did not work.

A new member of the team has been recruited and is settling in well – The GC Index® was used during the recruitment process and prior to offering the position for affirmation of fit within the organisation.

James has managed to persuade and encourage better team working – all of the individuals now feel more valued and less afraid of embracing change.

James said:

"Having a greater awareness of my own approach and how this could be measured has helped so much to enable me to re-engage with my team, help them to embrace change, to not be frightened of the future. It has given me more confidence to develop characteristics that were out of my comfort zone. I feel it is helping me to become a more-rounded individual and a much better leader and coach for my team."

Angie said:

"Coaching individuals when there are issues around conflict and change can be challenging to get to the heart of the issues quickly. The GC Index® provides that framework to help individuals to clearly see where they shine, and those areas for development opportunities."

Angie's Biography
Angie has a wide range of experience in the areas of leadership, employee engagement and business strategy. She works to inspire and develop people to unlock their potential.

Evolution4Business is supporting individuals, teams and organisations, working with global businesses through to medium sized organisations.

 www.evolution4business.co.uk

6. On the move while growing at >20% each year

Coach: Bjorn Kirchdorfer, Senior Partner at Top Gun Ventures

Coaching Context
Ken is the Founder and CEO of a financial services company based in Dallas/ Ft. Worth.

As a Founder of this business, Ken has grown the company from zero to over $4 Billion in Assets Under Management (AUM), servicing over 7,500 clients with over 100 team members across 14 locations and four US states (Texas, Oklahoma, Arizona and California).

Ken's profile, delivered by The GC Index®, as shown below, shows he is a strong Game Changer. This was not surprising, given his track record of game-changing success. His profile also revealed his proclivity to see action within a strategic context, his Strategist profile.

During our coaching conversations, we explored the implications of his evident strengths and those of his Chief Operating Officer, David who had also completed The GC Index®. From these explorations, Ken could clearly see that he needed to bring in the sort of leadership that could deliver the business strategy through clear operational plans.

Coaching Themes

The key themes in our coaching conversations were:

1. Senior Leadership: bringing clarity to the sort of leadership the business needed to bring effective operational plans and procedures to deliver strategic objectives.

2. Ken's role: being clear about, and adapting to, what this change would mean for his role within the business.

Ken's leadership team had been working together for a long time and team members knew each other formally and informally. However, The GC Index® profiles of team members added an extra dimension to Ken's understanding of his team, along with a framework for considering the impact and contribution he needed from new hires.

As we considered new additions to his team, he could clearly anticipate, using The GC Index® framework, how the dynamics of the team and his role would, and needed to change.

Initially, Ken wanted his new Executive Vice President of Sales to complement him with Implementer and Polisher strengths but, with consideration, he decided to recruit a Strategist/Implementer, an individual who could understand his strategic thinking, shape it and then make it happen.

101

Initially the business was solely focused on business to consumer and 'operating the machine' to do that. As the new head of sales role was refined, there were also new areas of business, including business to business. This needed someone to refine the strategy as well as execute it.

Necessarily, Ken used our coaching conversations as a space to explore what he needed, in terms of people on his team, to take his business to the next level of performance. The GC Index® played an important role in this process, providing a language and framework for understanding the challenge of putting together a high performing leadership team and business.

Coaching Outcomes
Ken is now very clear that his value to the business is as an outward-facing CEO, managing the business' external stakeholders. His new hires have freed him up to focus on his strengths and take on that role.

Moreover, his understanding about the natural strengths of people on his team, which he got from using The GC Index®, has helped him to build effective relationships with new hires quickly. This has sped up the on-boarding process because both Ken and the new hires have transparency about everyone's role and how they are contributing to objectives.

Ongoing work includes coaching and workshops designed to facilitate exceptional team performance. We are now expanding the use of The GC Index® as we add a Vice President level marketing leader to the team. Lastly, the coaching will enter the enterprise-wide phase as we deliver workshops to share how The GC Index® framework can help teams to be more effective.

The GC Index® will also give new leaders a valuable snapshot of their team that would otherwise take months or even years to capture.

Ken said:

"Intuitively and subjectively, I feel that I knew myself as well as those closest to me day to day. However, finding the alignment with a key hire upfront will help me work with, and support them, much better as they on-board."

David said:

"The ability to look across the organisation and find pockets of hidden talent will allow us to motivate and extend the career paths of key employees as we continue to grow rapidly. Being able to leverage the strengths of Ken in a targeted way will make all of us much more efficient and effective."

Bjorn said:

"Being able to help our clients see both the individual and collective impact of any key player in the organisation enables us to be better advisors and partners in helping them take their business to the next level of growth."

"We were able to leverage The GC Index® as a common language to benchmark the talent gaps we collectively identified. Moreover, the power of the team became our focal point as we supported this client with not only singular candidate selection, but collectively as we were able to strategically address organisational development."

Bjorn's Biography
Bjorn is a subject matter expert in building highly effective teams for global business success. He has had more than two decades of experience prior to joining Top Gun Ventures in 2008.

 www.TopGunVentures.com

Coaching Me Coaching You   ...Ahaa

7. Inspiring a Career Path Change

Coach: Lee Lam, Disruptor Consultant and Founder of Lee Lam Consulting

Coaching Context
Elliot had worked in recruitment roles for the majority of his career in the City of London. When he asked for my help he was working in an internal recruitment role for a global financial services organisation. He was feeling frustrated and bored with his current role with a concern that he was losing energy for his work.

Coaching Objectives
When I started my work with him, Elliot had already begun discussions with his manager with a focus upon his next career move, a move that would exploit his experience and give him the challenge that he needed. They were struggling to make progress in answering this question.

Elliot knew that he needed a move and wanted to explore the opportunities that were, potentially, on offer. Some of these opportunities would take him on a very different career path. For example, he was considering moving into a technology role that would have meant an initial backwards step for learning and development, but then seemed to have greater future options. He was very conscious that he had the ability to do a number of things and wanted help exploring the possibilities in order to make the right decision.

He was also under time pressure to make a decision. The GC Index® seemed like the perfect tool to use – it provided him with an accessible and relevant framework for thinking about his choice.

We felt that determining his strengths and natural proclivities would help him understand whether the frustration he was experiencing in his current role is due to the work itself, the environment, or perhaps being in the wrong profession.

Coaching Themes

Elliot's profile, delivered by The GC Index®, as shown on page 108, was consistent with the view that he was, at that point in time, somewhat disengaged. His relatively low scores are typical of people who see themselves in transition but with a feeling of being 'stuck'.

Our discussions during coaching sessions confirmed that he was not inspired by his work and, when asked to become more strategic by his boss, he began to feel resentful.

Although his profile didn't suggest a particularly strong natural proclivity (a score of seven or above), through our discussions it became clear that he typically took on, and was energised by, the Implementer role. He liked and needed the sense of satisfaction that came with being clear about what was expected of him. He wanted to be trusted to deliver tangible outcomes.

107

We agreed that his general lack of frustration with his current role was 'masking' his natural Implementer strengths. He did not feel that he was having the impact at work that he wanted to have.

Once this was identified, our explorations revealed that there was a particular option, discussed with his manager, that suited him more than any of the others. Indeed, the other options would have required him to be more strategic. This is a proclivity that, as he recognised, was not part of his makeup and not something that energised him. Seeing and accepting that he was not suited to strategic roles was a relief as it made the decision a lot easier. He felt that he could now make a decision that was based on his own interests and motivations rather than the advice of well-meaning colleagues.

Coaching Outcomes

Elliot's profile brought focus to our coaching conversations. He was then able to use the insights about himself, his proclivities and his motivations in subsequent conversations with his manager.

These conversations enabled him and his manager to shape a role that played to his strengths and allowed him to own some key and tangible deliverables that reflected his experience and expertise; he would know exactly what was expected of him. The role also gave him an opportunity to develop his Play Maker skills and inclinations and this appealed to him.

Lee said:

"As a 'Disruptor Coach', I like looking at things from various angles, knowing that looking at a new perspective can create significant and lasting change. The GC Index® allows me to disrupt current thinking on an individual's behaviour or strengths, as well as providing a simple but highly effective vocabulary to explain the way we view our contribution to our team, our organisation, or the world in general.

"Whether I am working with an individual on a career choice, or with a team who need to become high performers as quickly as possible, I can use the information from The GC Index® to make fast and effective progress with my clients and the individuals I coach."

Lee's Biography
Lee instigates real change for people, teams and business. She spent over 20 years in the financial technology industry before moving into consultancy working with established businesses to help them move with the times, as well as start ups who need a structured operation as quickly as possible.

 www.leelam.co.uk

8. Preparing for Partnership

Coach: Dr John Mervyn-Smith, Chief Psychologist at The GC Index.

Coaching Context
Naresh was a Director in a global consulting firm who was in his early 40s. He had been with the Firm for ten years and was highly regarded. He specialised in consulting on, and leading, IT enabled business transformation programmes.

He was seen to have partnership potential and he asked me to work with him to prepare him for the partner selection process and his transition to Partner, should he be successful.

Coaching Objectives
The main aim of our coaching relationship was to help Naresh to make a successful transition to partnership.

He was loyal to the consulting firm, and respected for it, but he felt that he career had stalled; his was ambitious and keen to progress to partnership.

We agreed upon a twelve-month coaching programme to help him realise his ambitions.

Coaching Themes
At the outset of the coaching programme we used The GC Index® as part of the process of establishing some concrete and detailed

111

objectives. His GC Index® profile is presented on page 113.

Naresh had a reputation within the firm for reliably delivering practical solutions that met the needs of his clients. This reputation is reflected in his profile, which was delivered by The GC Index®. More specifically, and consistent with his high Implementer score, he brought a very pragmatic approach to 'fixing' client issues and problems. He did so with energy and urgency, and clients and colleagues alike saw him as a 'safe pair of hands'. Moreover, when it mattered, he would deliver to the highest possible standard – his Polisher inclination. He is a proud individual who did not want to let himself or others down.

As we reviewed the demands of partnership, it became readily apparent to him that this ' hands-on approach' to leadership would put him under pressure as a partner. Partnership would mean a more outward-facing approach with a much greater focus upon business development, networking and thought leadership. He knew that he had to 'free' himself from too much 'hands-on' delivery lest he get 'bogged down' in the detail.

The first key theme of the coaching programme then was to review the ways in which Naresh needed to adapt his approach to make time for partner activities. In part, this meant developing the practical skills for effective performance management: delegating and holding others to account. In a psychological sense it also meant learning how to 'let go', not something that people with Polisher inclinations find easy. They can easily feel let down by others who do not 'live up to' their standards.

The second theme, consistent with his firm's reputation in its markets, was about taking 'leading edge' and innovative solutions to its clients. Naresh, consistent with some of the comments above was a cautious individual, he valued the pragmatic and the 'tried and tested'. He knew that he would not be the source of creativity in his team but he also knew that he could recruit and nurture creative talent. Overall, he knew that making the very best of the talent in his team – being the Play Maker – was good for the firm and good for him as a partner.

Coaching Outcomes

Clarity about how he would need to be an effective partner, helped Naresh to make adjustments before the partner selection process began and to present with confidence during it. He also grew in confidence as he took on the outward facing duties of a partner.

Naresh was made partner nine months ago and, through his contributions to the firm, feels that he is amongst peers with his partners.

Naresh said:

"I like the language and the framework provided by The GC Index®. It gives me a very simple way of focusing upon being an effective leader and partner."

John's Biography
John has over 30 years' experience assessing leadership capabilities, and coaching senior executives and their teams to deliver impact. He has a particular interest in leadership development and emotional resilience.

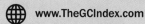 **www.TheGCIndex.com**

9. You're not always behaving the way you think you are; or need to be

Coach: Mike O'Dell, Business Advisor & Executive Coach

Coaching Context
My Coachee, Jim, was in his mid-50s and was in transition from one style of working to another. He had decided it was time to create his own consulting business, with an emphasis on supporting technology-based firms through culture change and providing coaching services.

Jim had a background in accounting and marketing, leading to him becoming General Manager and CEO of mid-sized biotech firms. He had been used to having a team around him, leading and directing progress and actions with an approach that reflected his strong values – honesty, trust, openness and collaboration.

Coaching Objectives
Jim felt that he wasn't getting the pace and traction he needed for his business, despite the subject area being a real passion of his. Additionally, he was becoming frustrated and irritated in his dealings with clients and potential partners, so he sought my help as a means of identifying what he needed to do differently.

115

Coaching Themes

As part of the coaching process, I asked Jim to complete The GC Index®.

Surprisingly, his profile, as shown below, highlighted low scores across all five proclivities. The top score was for Strategist, but only rating a four. His next highest score was a two for Game Changer, with the remainder scoring one.

'Flat' profiles, such as this, typically suggest that an individual, at that point in time, is very low on energy and drive when it comes to the world of work.

I fed this profile back to Jim. Initially, it elicited a negative and rejecting response. He believed he was significantly stronger across all proclivities, but especially on strategy, game-changing and play-making.

After some discussion, I encouraged him to explore why he thought that any of his scores should be different. In particular, I encouraged him to use The GC Index® framework to think about how he saw himself in his previous leadership role(s) compared to his current consulting/advisory role.

During this exploration, it became increasingly apparent that he lacked focus and energy for his current consulting role. Jim realised that without a clear focus – the Strategist in his nature – he quickly loses energy.

This discussion allowed us to raise the obvious question for Jim: "Is my current role/environment suited to my proclivities and energies?"

Jim rapidly 'locked onto' this question, which freed him to explore his career needs and motivations. As Coach, I took on the role of 'sounding-board' and reflector to help him to hone his thoughts and growing insights.

During our conversations he developed a much greater sense of awareness of his needs and motivations. With this growing awareness, he became energised and focused. He produced an action plan that we would implement and track as part of our coaching relationship. The essence of the plan was to test his decision to make a career move, keeping open the option of a more 'traditional' career and, with it, the roles he had been used to which had brought him success.

Together we created a short 13-point action plan, which included:

- Articulate and live a "galvanising purpose" – so he could be clear what he wanted to achieve.

- Stop vacillating and procrastinating – get down and do things!

- Set and meet specific near-term targets designed to make the business progress.

- To be himself: to take feedback positively without needing to "bend like the willow or hold fast like the oak" every time.

117

We used our subsequent coaching sessions to track and review progress, to refine and add goals and to discuss what worked well and what didn't.

Coaching Outcomes

To date, Jim is 'motoring' and building his business actively and with significantly more enthusiasm and enjoyment. He has recognised that he can't behave as a CEO with his clients, who often are the CEO, and that he isn't coaching if he is 'telling people what to do'.

The situation remains a work in progress, but one which is very firmly based on successfully re-energising Jim and supporting him in re-affirming his motivations and capabilities.

Mike said:

"I value the insight offered by The GC Index® as it provides a useful perspective on what people are like, in behavioural terms, when they are at their best. It gives more than just a description of someone's personality.

It creates an insightful basis on which to structure a coaching conversation about how one can apply and focus proclivities and energies in any given situation and can help you understand how best to get the most from oneself and colleagues."

Mike's Biography
Mike has over 20 years' experience working with leading technology companies, as well as having worked within executive search and consultancy. Mike has had consistent success in shaping and delivering change to a variety of organisations in fast moving, international businesses spanning much of the globe.

 www.linkedin.com/in/mike-o-dell-b0606b2

10. Sharing the Skill – Creating the Dream

Coach: Gaylin Jee, Founder and Strategist at 33 Emeralds

Coaching Context

Mia is a performing artist with an enviable track record, having produced five albums and released nine singles to radio. She was invited to sing for Nelson Mandela's 80th and 82nd birthdays (where she met Bono from U2 – but didn't realise who he was at the time!), performing at the Olympic Stadium in Barcelona, and doing the "Rocking Future" roadshow promoting anti-bullying in 30 schools across South Africa.

In 2016 she launched a business called Sing-It. They offer private and group voice coaching, as well as a three to six year Little Blue Birds programme for early childhood learners, thus activating a lifelong love of music.

Mia is taking her remarkable talents a step further by creating opportunities for young, aspiring singers and those artists with a purpose beyond performing. She has developed the accredited "Sing-It Syllabus". Performing artists can train to use her syllabus to teach people of any age to sing, sharing the joy of music, doing what they love, and earning an income at the same time.

Coaching Objectives

Mia is highly passionate and driven. Her Sing-It Syllabus is being implemented in four schools in South

Africa and she has gutsy growth targets to extend this reach. She is already pursuing accreditation for the syllabus in Canada, where she plans to establish a business presence later in 2018.

Mia wanted to take stock of her plans for her career. She wanted my help as a Coach to think, in more detail, about how to build her digital presence, aligning it to her larger business purpose and plans.

Coaching Themes

Mia has strong Polisher and Game Changer inclinations as presented overleaf, complemented by high Strategist and Implementer proclivities. This suggests that Mia is flexible and adaptable – she can contribute in many ways because her energy lies in many places. Mia has an ability to see a future that others don't (Game Changer), and a desire to answer the 'Why' as well as the 'How' (Strategist). She not only wants to get things done (Implementer), but she wants them to be perfect (Polisher). We see this high-energy profile reflected in her early achievements as a performing artist, and later through the launch of a business with global growth plans to 'share the skill and create the dream'.

Mia took The GC Index® as part of a small business impact programme run by 33 Emeralds. The GC Index® created a pause-point for Mia. With a focus on achieving her larger aspirations, Gaylin asked: "Given you only have so many hours in each day, where is your time best focussed so as to have most impact and to add optimal value to your business?"

The profile prompted Mia to take stock of what is most important right now, and what elements she needs to drive personally. These themes were at the heart of the coaching relationship. She needed to decide what to 'let go of', what to 'park for now', and what to delegate.

Given that her energy does not lie in play making, we also discussed who in her circles could bring this contribution to the business. They could be instrumental in assisting her to recruit and train new voice Coaches to roll out the business model, and could also provide assistance in building the team to run a successful operation in South Africa as Mia expands to Canada.

Mia has recently recruited a new team member into the business, and her profile offers Implementer with balanced scores on all other roles. As the new team member grows into her role, we hope that she will effectively assist with getting prioritised business ideas actioned, freeing up some of Mia's time and energy for developing other aspects of the business.

Mia can be a "Tour de Force". This is how leading edge change is driven. We acknowledged how important it is to 'take others with you', to communicate your vision and to inspire others – not everyone immediately 'gets' a bigger purpose or picture.

Coaching Outcomes

For Mia to maximise her impact, she is learning to balance her focus and time. In particular, identifying priorities for the immediate future and focusing on them, letting go of some of the 'smaller stuff', and on-boarding people who are best placed to 'lift the load'. This is hard for her but predictably so given her profile, delivered by The GC Index®.

Mia is building her digital presence and letting the world know what she is passionate about, as well as how they can get involved. She plans to be operating from Canada later this year, once Sing-It has established an impactful presence in South Africa. And she is laying a solid, focused foundation to achieve that. With The GC Index®, she now knows how to apply her strengths to make what she has been dreaming about for years a reality.

Mia said:

"Thanks Gaylin. You are such a star! I really appreciate all your help in getting me to focus on what is important and where I can ask for help."

Gaylin said:

"Mia's view of the future is big, and the desire to realise it so strong. These passionate people are the ones who change the way things get done. It is inspirational to share in the vision to help everybody make their game-changing impact, and to be able to offer practical tools like The GC Index® that help to make it all happen."

Gaylin's Biography

Gaylin runs 33 Emeralds, a niche consultancy based in South Africa. She focuses on stretching minds and comfort zones with disruptive thinking and practical tools, such as The GC Index®. Her goal is to help everyone to craft a better working future for themselves, and for the people around them.

 www.thirtythreeemeralds.com

Appendix:

The GC Index® – Roles and Capabilities: Strategist

Appendix 1

Proclivity	Leadership Role	Core Capabilities	Key Skills
		'Reading Signals'	• Being able to observe patterns and trends in your world, knowing what's relevant and what's noise in relevant world • Suspending judgment while 'collecting data'; hearing as well as listening • Well developed analytical skills for testing assumptions about data and the possible patterns and trends within data
Strategist	'To engage others with a clear direction that brings focus to action'	'Evaluating Possibilities'	• Being able to understand the context and criteria for choosing between different possibilities • Suspending judgment while 'collecting data'; hearing as well as listening • Well developed analytical skills for testing assumptions about data and the possible patterns and trends within it

	'Engaging and Influencing'	· Articulating a clear picture of the present that supports a compelling vision for the future
		· Being able to articulate, and present with clarity, an argument with implications for action
		· Communication skills such as being able to 'engage hearts and minds'
		· Being open to the influence of others

Notes:

Appendix 1

The GC Index® – Roles and Capabilities: Game Changer

Proclivity	Leadership Role	Core Capabilities	Key Skills
Game Changer	'To generate ideas and possibilities that have the potential to be transformational'	'Being Creative'	• Understanding how the creative process works for you and creating environments that are conducive to creativity • Being clear with others about what you need from them to be creative • Making time to be creative, to be inspired, to 'obsess'
		'Building Alliances'	• Building support in those relationships (especially boss) that will give you the freedom to be creative • Building complementary relationships with colleagues who can help you to evaluate and articulate your ideas and turn them into a reality

	'Engaging and Influencing'	• Helping others to see what you see • Understanding and managing others' resistance to transformational possibilities • Communication/presentation skills • Establish authority as the basis for influence, such as building a track record of turning ideas into tangible outcomes

Notes:

The GC Index® – Roles and Capabilities: Play Maker

Proclivity	Leadership Role	Core Capabilities	Key Skills
Play Maker	'To get the best from others, individually and collectively, in support of agreed goals and objectives'	'Getting the Best from Others'	• Organisational intelligence: understanding what is needed, in terms of people capability, to get a task done • Emotional intelligence: being insightful about what motivates people to be at their best • Recognising and valuing the talents of others
		'Building Trust and Community'	• Building trusting relationships based upon personal integrity • Building supportive networks of people • Brokering relationships in a way that helps others to build their networks • Being a role model for inclusive behaviours

Appendix 1

	'Engaging and Influencing'	• Facilitating debate and consensus • Being a role model for openness to influence • Effectively managing conflict and the potential for conflict • Being prepared to be directive when it's appropriate • Effectively managing complex stakeholder relationships

Notes:

131

The GC Index® – Roles and Capabilities: Implementer

Appendix 1

Proclivity	Leadership Role	Core Capabilities	Key Skills
Implementer	'To shape strategic plans and deliver tangible outcomes'	'Evaluating Strategy' 'Effective delivery'	• Understanding the Strategist's role and accepting that they will generate possibilities, some of which aren't practical, feasible and feasible with modification • Asking the questions that can, constructively, evaluate the operational feasibility of strategic possibilities • Transforming strategy into tangible, feasible, and realistic operational action plans
		'Engaging and Influencing'	• Making sure that actions are aligned to strategic objectives • Knowing what the priorities are for action and bringing focus to action • Knowing when to be ' hands-on'; delegating effectively • Bringing energy, urgency, and focus to action • Holding others to account for their performance

- Understanding and managing others' resistance to change
- Being a role model for positive action
- Communication/presentation skills
- Establish authority as the basis for influence, typically, credibility that comes from effective delivery

Notes:

The GC Index® – Roles and Capabilities: Polisher

Appendix 1

Proclivity	Leadership Role	Core Capabilities	Key Skills
		'Being Innovative'	• Making time to be innovative, to be inspired, to 'obsess'
			• Make sure that you are in a team/organisation that values learning, continuous improvements and innovation
			• Make time for your own personal and professional development
Polisher	To be the guardian of learning, continuous improvement and the 'pursuit of excellence'	'Delivering Tangible Outcomes'	• Be sure that when you focus your efforts, they are aligned with broader business goals
			• Know when something is good enough; learn not to over-deliver when you don't need to
			• Know when to 'cut your losses' if something isn't working
			• Recognise when you are being too 'tough' on yourself and demanding of others

	'Engaging and Influencing'	<ul><li>Learn how to 'sell' your ideas, adapting to your audience</li><li>Make sure you understand and can articulate the business context for change/innovation</li><li>Polishers can be critical - seek to inspire with your striving for excellence rather than inhibiting</li><li>Make time for your own personal and professional development - your expertise will underpin your ability to influence</li></ul>

Notes:

Appendix 2 –
The Psychology
of The GC Index® :
Strategist

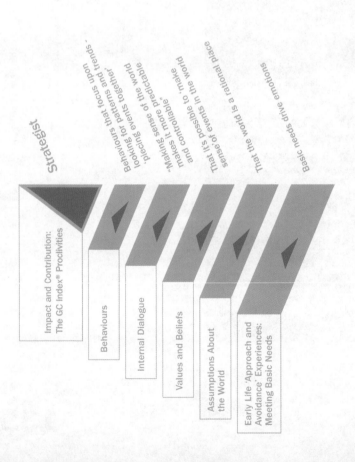

Strategist

Behaviours that focus upon trends - looking for patterns and trends - 'piecing events together'

"Making sense of the world makes it more predictable and controllable to 'make sense of events in the world

That it's possible to 'make sense of events in the world

That the world is a rational place

Basic needs drive emotions

Impact and Contribution: The GC Index® Proclivities

Behaviours

Internal Dialogue

Values and Beliefs

Assumptions About the World

Early Life 'Approach and Avoidance' Experiences: Meeting Basic Needs

Appendix 2 – The Psychology of The GC Index® : Game Changer

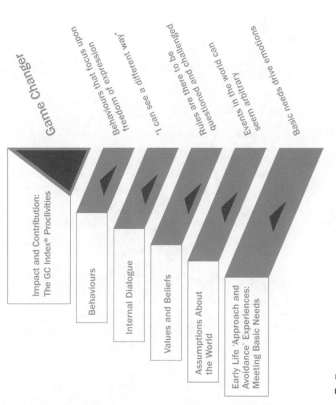

Game Changer

- Behaviours that focus upon freedom of expression
- "I can see a different way"
- Rules are there to be questioned and challenged
- Events in the world can seem arbitrary
- Basic needs drive emotions

- Impact and Contribution: The GC Index® Proclivities
- Behaviours
- Internal Dialogue
- Values and Beliefs
- Assumptions About the World
- Early Life 'Approach and Avoidance' Experiences: Meeting Basic Needs

Appendix 2 – The Psychology of The GC Index®: Play Maker

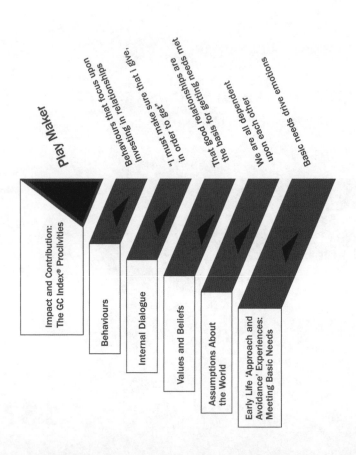

Play Maker

Impact and Contribution: The GC Index® Proclivities

Behaviours — Behaviours that focus upon investing in relationships

Internal Dialogue — "I must make sure that I give, in order to get"

Values and Beliefs — That good relationships are the basis for getting needs met

Assumptions About the World — We are all dependent upon each other

Early Life 'Approach and Avoidance' Experiences: Meeting Basic Needs — Basic needs drive emotions

Appendix 2 – The Psychology of The GC Index®: Implementer

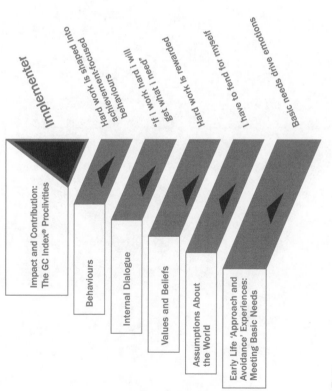

Implementer

- Impact and Contribution: The GC Index® Proclivities
- Behaviours — Hard work is shaped into achievement-focused behaviours
- Internal Dialogue — "If I work hard I will get what I need"
- Values and Beliefs — Hard work is rewarded
- Assumptions About the World — I have to fend for myself
- Early Life 'Approach and Avoidance' Experiences: Meeting Basic Needs — Basic needs drive emotions

Appendix 2 –
The Psychology
of The GC Index® :
Polisher

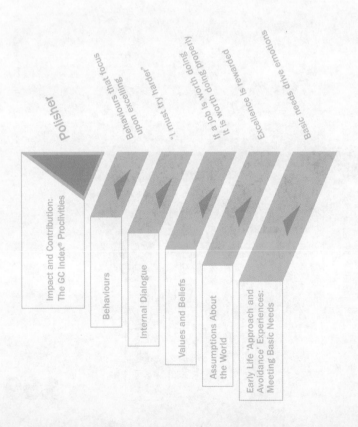

Polisher

Behaviours that focus upon excelling

"I must try harder"

If a job is worth doing it is worth doing properly

Excellence is rewarded

Basic needs drive emotions

Impact and Contribution: The GC Index® Proclivities

Behaviours

Internal Dialogue

Values and Beliefs

Assumptions About the World

Early Life 'Approach and Avoidance' Experiences: Meeting Basic Needs

Appendix 3 – Multi-Dimensional Leadership

Contemporary Leaders

Creative Leaders

Visionary Leaders

Leaders as Coaches

Pragmatic Leaders

Inspirational Leaders

Charismatic Leaders

Leaders by Example

Inventive Leaders

Aspirational Leaders

KEY:

 Strategist Game Changer Play Maker Implementer Polisher

For clarification:
These individuals haven't undertaken The GC Index® and their alignment with the respective leadership combination is an educated estimation to help bring the concept of 'Multi-Dimensional Leadership' to life for others.

Bibliography

1   Esser, J.K. (1998). Alive and Well after 25
    years: A review of groupthink research.
    Organizational Behavior & Human
    Decision Processes, 73 (2-3), 116-141.

2   McCracken, H. How Gmail Happened:
    The Inside Story of Its Launch 10 Years
    Ago. Time. 1st April 2014.

3   Ott, N. & Mervyn-Smith, J (2015). The
    DNA of a Game Changer. London, eg.1.

4   Dyson, J; Coren, G (1997). Against
    The Odds (1st ed.). London, UK: Orion
    Publishing. ISBN 0-7528-0981-4.

5   Fox, J J; Reiss, R (2012). The
    Transformative CEO: Impact Lessons
    From Industry Game Changers.
    McGraw-Hill. ISBN 9780071794985.

6   Ott, N. & Mervyn-Smith, J (2016). The
    DNA of a Game-Changing Team. London,
    eg.1.

7   Hersey, P. and Blanchard, K. (1969).
    'Lifecycle of Leadership'. Training and
    Development Journal 23 (5): 26-34.

8   Fernandez, C.F., and Vecchio, R. P. (1997).
    Situational leadership theory revisited:
    A test of an across-jobs perspective.
    The Leadership Quarterly, 8 (1), 67-84.

9   Bennis, W. and Nanus, B. (1985).
     Leaders: Strategies for Taking Charge.
     New York, Harper Row.

10   Rogers, C. (1951). Client-Centered
     Therapy.

11   Tojeiro, K (2015). The Art of Possible.
     ISBN: 993236901

143